Songs For Lola

JK Grande

BookLeaf Publishing
India | USA | UK

Presentation by *BookLeaf Publishing*

Web: www.bookleafpub.com

E-mail: info@bookleafpub.com

ISBN: 9789358737028

First edition 2023

*To my family, my brothers who raised me
and my children who made me grow.*

How Can I Love You?

Can I love you to fix you?
To have that power to make you grow
To steal your anger when rage starts to flow.

Can I love you to help you?
To breakdown the problems that muddy your
mind
To bring method to madness when you're
stumbling blind

Can I love you to heal you?
For all the times you've felt wrong
When they said you were broken and didn't
belong

Can I love you to show you?
That you're worthy of this
That the life that I gave you can offer such bliss

Can you love you like I do?
When the shadows are playing games in your
head
And the darkness has gathered you up in your
bed
Can you love you? Love you, like I do.

Within Prayer

Be kind to your child full of fear and wonder
Be kind to your wounded soldier battle worn
Be kind to your adult just coping in the eye of
the storm, still holding on
In the softness of heart your mind will see and
create

Where We Come From

My tears are frozen
in memories too painful to thaw
I'm ice to the core
Waiting for the next phone call

We're on this road now
There's no good on this path
Where are our happy endings?
We never had none, don't be daft

Cos kids like us just grow wrong
There's no happy ending where we come from

My Brother

My brother loves to run
He runs so fast
He'll run forever
To hell and back
Just to bring me a flower
To make me smile

How long you gonna run this time?
When will you be back?
Your bodies broken
Just stop, let it go

Hell is your home
And few know it like you
But, you need to come home now
You need to come home now

Call

All the space that sits between us
Thinking of your face when you smile
I don't know when we'll be together
Let me hold some hope for a while

Can you call for me
When it's all on me
Now I'm fighting through the night
I need you to come to me
When it's all on me
Just lay your body down
With me

Days go by and I can't not think of you
I wonder if you think of me too
It feels like something is missing
And that something has to be you

Breathing

I'm breathing in all of you
This moment is going to pass
When it's over, it's done for forever
I hope we can make this last

Come lay your body down
Listen to my heart
Feel the breeze blow through the window
Watch the curtains dance

Don't pull your clothes on yet
I like how they look on the floor
Give me more of this moment to linger
Hold your body against mine for longer
I'm always gonna want more

Abandon

I give everything
You want more
I'm tired, I'm empty
But you want more
I'm sick, I'm crying
You want more
I'm leaving, I'm broken
But you want more
I've lost myself
You want more
Do you see me?
Give me more
What am I doing?
They want more
I can't keep going!
Give me more
Can I leave?
I'm so alone
So many things I need to be
I can't remember being me

Him

Eyes closed, my cheek to yours
Prickly hairs like pins, pierce my skin
It hurts to love you
You're warm, softness around your eyes
I smile and peak, just for a moment
You're looking at me
Say nothing
Poker faced
What are you thinking?
What are you feeling?
The breeze reminds me the world is out there
Our bubble bursts
I close my eyes and press myself against you
Bury my face in your neck
Breath, breath his smell
My arms stretched around his waist
Hold on
Just hold on
The world is out there.

Please Ignore

Please ignore
The way I move around her
Please ignore
My staring when she speaks
Please ignore
The messages I send her
Please ignore
My missing cuff links
Please ignore
The nights I spend away from you
Please ignore
The absence of mystique
Please ignore
Every word I tell you
Please ignore
The fact that you're so weak

Witches

Circling the seasons
Searching for the moonlight
Casting spells for love

The Verb

Who were you to love me?
To pick me up from the floor
Then placed yourself above me
"Isn't that what love is for?"

I don't want to fix you
I am not your fan
Go seek out another
For your sordid plan

Who were you to love me?
Always playing to the crowd
Leaving wasn't easy
Now my freedom is allowed

"Please, don't leave me!
Fall back under my spell"
I'm going cos I realised
You cannot love me well.

Amaru

Goodbye to the rose
Farewell angel flower
Somewhere in your rest
I hope that you find power

Goodbye sacred words
Spoken in your voice
A rising that is cursed
Where women have no choice

The concrete that we walk
Will break below our feet
Uprising comes a stalk
The flowers smell so sweet

We'll wake you oh, so gently
And tell the day has come
Now freedom is upon you
Love has finally won

Shame in Desire

In your smile
Beauty lays
I'll stare and while

I compile
All the ways
You seemingly beguile

Loving hurts in every style
The heart sways
Around again, a nubile

Counterpoints are virile
Our bodies obey
Ashamed, I hide in exile

The Delusionist's Wife

Are you a bit like me?
Or, has my vision gone askew?
With your left and my right
We could tie a shoe

I can make a home in here
A space that's shaped to you
A lilly for a rose
In lakes of purest blue

The months are passing by
My dreams aren't coming true
You're standing in the snow
Cold and looking for me too

Dis-association

15

Behind grey veils, I'm hard to follow
Here today and gone tomorrow
Staring away, feeling hollow
She's lost again, here comes the sorrow

Please, know that I still love you
Even when I'm gone
This time won't last forever
It's dark before the dawn

Ashamed to be so distant
This heart beats warm not cold
Green peaches soften slowly
Then duly turn sweet gold

Young McQuesten

There was a young lad called McQuesten
He wasn't much into resting
He danced so obscene
The gals were too keen
So the police had to come and arrest him

Adult Child

Will you come to this gig
I don't want to go alone
Actually, I changed my mind
I'd rather stay home

There's the guy I mentioned
Don't look he might see
I'm gonna go talk to him
No, actually I'll just let it be

I just bought some tap shoes
I want to give it a go
I saw them laughing
I learn too slow

I know you think I'm silly
Like I'm stumbling blind
But I'm trying to give a chance
To the kid inside my mind

It's not easy
When everyone's ahead
I'm back to the drawing board
Back to the shed

At the arse end of nowhere
Book and pencil in hand
I can say one thing
This was not what I planned

Normal

You're probably not normal
Because you came from me
You know the old saying
The apple and the tree

So what, you're different
With your curls or orange hair
You're sweet and magic
Let yourself dare

Take your place in this world
Show your flare and be bold
This time isn't forever
One day you'll be old

There'll be good days and bad ones
And, some people won't get you
But the ones that do matter
Won't ever forget you

The Bump

One more wriggle
One more hiccup
In my bump while oils I apply
One last bout of brutal indigestion
Before we part our ties

One more stumble
One more cuddle
One more gummy smile
I said I'd keep a diary
But, I was tired all the while

One more dance
One more story
One more hero quest
You're off to school tomorrow
Finally can rest

Please stop yelling
Please stop saying
You can't wait to be free
My heart hurts cos you're trying
To break away from me

One more biscuit

One more cuddle
When do you think you'll call?
I know you're really busy
You might not call at all

Where did all the time go?
You're suddenly in flight
I can't believe you're off!
I hope I did it right.

Abbi's Limerick

There was a tall woman called Abbi
She always dressed well, never shabby
Men's knees would go weak
As her chest brushed their cheek
So she had to hail them a cabby

Spiders

Spiders in the autumn
Make me think of you
"Don't be afraid Jessie"
They're not concerned with you
I found your little tote bag
The logo 'Slytherin'
You, always an outsider
Didn't want to be let in
A face with so much beauty
A smile like the stars
Although, you didn't feel it
Deep down too many scars
We found your empty bottles
We drowned in all your gin
You pulled us all down with you
Then left us in a spin
Now life goes on without you
The seasons come and go
I wonder, did you love me?
I guess I'll never know
Now all I have is spiders
To bring back memories
I loved you, I forgive you
I hope that you're at ease.